10 MOONS AND 13 HORSES

WESTERN LITERATURE SERIES

T0097668

GARY SHORT

10 MOONS AND 13 HORSES

UNIVERSITY OF NEVADA PRESS ▲▲ RENO & LAS VEGAS

P O E M S

Western Literature Series

University of Nevada Press,

Reno, Nevada 89557 USA

www.upress.nevada.edu

Copyright © 1994, 1996, 1998, 1999,

2000, 2001, 2002, 2003, 2004 by

Gary Short

Manufactured in the United States

of America

Design by Carrie House

LIBRARY OF CONGRESS CATALOGING-IN-

PUBLICATION DATA

Short, Gary, 1953–

10 moons and 13 horses : poems /

Gary Short.

p. cm. — (Western literature series)

ISBN 978-0-87417-583-7 (pbk. : alk.

paper)

1. Place (Philosophy)—Poetry.

2. Violence—Poetry. 3. Deserts—Poetry.

4. Nevada—Poetry. 5. Family—Poetry.

I. Title: Ten moons and thirteen horses.

II. Title. III. Series.

PS3569.H588a613   2004

811'.54—DC22   2003022018

The paper used in this book meets the

requirements of American National

Standard for Information Sciences—

Permanence of Paper for Printed

Library Materials, ANSI Z.48-1984.

Binding materials were selected for

strength and durability.

The book has been reproduced
as a digital reprint.

FOR BURNETT AND MIMI MILLER
FOR JON CHRISTENSEN AND KIT MILLER

CONTENTS

ACKNOWLEDGMENTS

Grateful acknowledgments are made to the following magazines in which some of these poems first appeared:

Antioch Review: "Herida de Amor" and "Imperfect History" as a section of the poem "The Giant Ants of Texas"
Blue Mesa Review: "Aperture"
Isle: "Ghost Dance" and "Sheep and Stars"
Luna: "Perseid Shower"
Onthebus: "Junk Cars: Mina, Nevada"
Permafrost: "Brothers Playing Catch on Christmas Day"
Ploughshares: "Sway"
Poetry: "Breath" and "I Lay My Brother Down"
Puerto del Sol: "Teaching Poetry to 3rd Graders" and "What I Believed"
Quarterly West: "Outlines"
Wild Duck Review: "American Flat"
Willow Springs: "Command," "Nesting" and "Release"

Some of these poems appeared in the chapbooks *Imperfect History* (Midnight Sun Editions) and *Desire* (Black Rock Press). "Brothers Playing Catch on Christmas Day" was published in *Theory of Twilight* (Ahsahta Press). "Outlines" also appeared on the *Poetry Daily* Web site (*www.poems.com*).

Many thanks to Catherine French, Caroline Finkelstein, Marianne Botos, Norman Dubie, Sandra Alcosser, Sean Nevin, Astrid Maria Rodas, Luljeta Lleshanaku, Scott Slovic, and Melisa Cahnmann.

I would like to express my appreciation to Stanford University for a Wallace Stegner Fellowship; the MacDowell Colony, the Vermont Studio Center, and Virginia Center for the Creative Arts for residencies; and the Nevada Arts Council and the Sierra Arts Foundation for grants support. This book was completed at Lynchburg College in Virginia while I was the Thornton Writer-in-Residence.

1

Outlines

I hear Jon in the yard with his two small daughters who trace
their bodies in chalk on the patio. The shapes are
biomorphic, scrawled in green on pink pavement.
The girls ask Jon for help. He takes the chalk.
"All right," he says, "I'll draw the outline and then
you have to fill yourself in.

In the barn. The wood, the dust, and horse sweat. It all
smells good like old books. We surprise an owl. It is white
as moon and flies back and forth among the rafters and
spangles of floating chaff. Back and forth like a trapped
soul.

Why I like reading in the center of night by a dim light—
only the words in the book are illumined. Darkness around
the edges of the page. Last night reading William Maxwell
at age 89, saying, "People die and then they're gone. I will
never get used to it."

An autumn memory. Helping my mother gather leaves
from the cottonwood and poplar. The rule is
we have to catch them in mid-air as they spin
from the trees. Afterward, my mother scotch-tapes
those yellow leaves to the bare trees of a painted landscape
hanging above the cat-scratched couch.

Once a blind woman, my student, asked if she could touch
my face. In her reaching, I felt a bridge. Her fingertips
pressed, more firm than I expected, repeatedly, in silence.
Then she sighed. "That's what I thought," she said.

There was a man, a tourist from Michigan, who died alone
in a motorcycle accident at the abandoned silver mill
a mile from my home. The sheriff told me he'd been paralyzed
but conscious for awhile. When he died, I was the nearest
person to him.

I recall the spaces between the falling leaves. Vacant
air and shape that stayed in place for only
a moment.

When my mother died, I took several pairs of her dress shoes
with the idea of giving them away. But the dog
got into the back of the truck and scattered them
from the cowpond to the asphalt road. I went walking
in the valley and saw a magpie, black/white, in the
sage—breathless, still. I moved closer and realized
it was my mother's shoe, a sleek two-toned spectator pump.

At the post office the teenage boy ahead of me, holding an envelope
with the note or letter sealed inside, requests a stamp.
The woman behind the counter says, "Would you like peaches,
flags, or love?"

I looked for some evidence of the man's dying
down by the old mill. A blood-stained rock
or a chalked police-drawn body.

What I found in the dust was the papery husk
of a snake. Imagine that, to leave your skin
without leaving your body.

Brothers Playing Catch on Christmas Day

Only a little light remains.
The new football feels heavy
and our throws are awkward
like the conversation of brothers
who see each other occasionally.
After a few exchanges,
confidence grows,
the passing and catching
feels natural and good.
Gradually, we move farther apart,
out in the field,
the space between us
filling with darkness.

He leads me,
lofting perfect spirals
into the night. My eyes
find the clean white laces of the ball.
I let fly a deep pass
to his silhouette.
The return throw
cannot be seen,
yet the ball
falls into my hands, as if
we have established a code
that only brothers know.

I Lay My Brother Down

The day before he dies
I lift him,
while the nurse works
coiled and crimped tubes
that run from his body,
a tangle of exterior veins.

The white sun breaks through the window,
takes the room and clarifies
shadows the simple poplar limbs make
on the hospital wall. The leaves are all gone.
The leaves and color are gone.
It hurts,

his bones sharp against my chest,
the lightness of him, his body
lucid and thinned
to this shaking weight.
A ninety-pound dying man.
Tomorrow he'll be gone.

My brother's eyes are closed.
I pull closer.
I want to hold him
in this world.
His hair brushes my cheek.
I lay my brother down

on the white sheet. My brother
opens his eyes
and sees shadows, sparrows on the wall
flocking to the bare limbs
of the poplar. "Look at that,"
he says and points,

"The leaves are returning to the tree."

Aperture

From behind the screen door I watch the cat
in the bunchgrass stalking at dusk.
With the pure attention of religion,
he waits for the skitter of a field mouse,
a shiver in an owl's dream.

The cat delivers his limp prey
to the chipped gray paint of the porch.
I step outside, not knowing
if I will punish the cat
or accept the mouse.

At the edge of the porch I kneel and see
the map of red capillaries
in the delicate mouse ear.

I lift it by the tail to toss,
but in the blink of a smug cat's eye
I feel a tug—an escape
back into life.

In the African journals, Livingston tells
of the charging lion that knocked him down.
When he was held in the lion's mouth,
the human body's trance-like response
was to go limp in an ecstatic giving up
that saved. To assume death

to stay alive.

A Confederate soldier at Antietam
played dead when his battalion was overrun.
for a moment he thought he was safe,
but to make sure, the Union infantryman
drove a bayonet into each body on the ground.

When I pick up the mouse
and it jerks from terror-induced sleep,
I feel all that fear
in a small heartbeat.

My panicked fingers let go
and the mouse slips into the brush where it may be
safe for awhile. Though the cat
is all tension now and ready
to pounce again. I shut him in the house,

stand on the porch and watch the first stars
burn holes in the sky.
Dark enlarging around me,
the pupil in a cat's eye.

Ghost Dance

This fall the pine nuts are sparse in the piñons.
Some say the bad year
is the residual of drought. Others blame
a plague of tiny spiders
that invaded the woody cones.

When the wind moves there are voices
through the trees that border the Paiute cemetery
in Schurz, Nevada. Once I watched
a large crow lift

from a headstone. The bird was shadow
unfolding over hills of red dust.
Its wings were black prisms.

Rae Rae Antelope told me another reason
for this fall's bad harvest—the Pine Nut Ceremony
failed. Two elders died
last summer. Now

no one knows the full dance or song.
The words are lost. When they tried
to call up the song, an enormous wind
spiraled ghosts of dust and sand.

The people ran, leaving one young man
in a reddish cloud
dancing haltingly around the piñon tree.

At the Paiute cemetery at dusk, I stand
near Wovoka's grave—Wovoka,
who dreamed the Ghost Dance, a ritual
to restore the world. The vision

swept over the plains from here to Dakota.
A belief that if the Indians danced
long and hard enough the dead would live

and the old ways return. Looking west
into the lowering light I see a young man
wearing the local high school football jersey.

He kneels at a grave site. I can't see
his bowed head but clearly read the "42"
on his back in blue script. I step toward him

then realize it's a shirt pulled tight
over the inverted U of the tombstone,
a teenager buried there
just two weeks before.

I lose my place, have to begin
to understand all over again.

In an Episcopal church performance
of Arthur Kopit's *Indians*
at the Pyramid Lake Reservation,
I play the part of a reporter interviewing a general
on the killing field
that was the massacre at Wounded Knee Creek,

where the rounded-up Lakota Sioux had danced
on and on into trance, chanting,
"We will live again, we will."
The cavalry soldiers panicked
and killed. Hundreds dead in the snow.

When the lights dim
dozens of Indian children in the audience
rush to the front of the sanctuary
and lay their bodies down
in a frozen depiction of slaughter.

So many bodies
piled near the altar;
I can't keep my balance
stepping among the tangled arms.

One girl looks up
and winks to reassure, but I feel
a chill—late December, South Dakota,

1890, or just yesterday,
alone in a cemetery in Nevada.
It's hard times when a young man appears
in the shape of a tombstone.

Junk Cars: Mina, Nevada

These cars traveled the road
you now travel
to get to another place.
They knew the hymn of tires, the wind
through grillwork and over fenders.
Hard-driven American models with names of birds
or Indian chiefs.
Up on blocks now in front of shacks
that flag from wind,
the cars hunch in isolation.
Nests of thistles work through floorboards
weaving metal to earth.

This is retribution—
things stalled that once moved.
Town of broken hearts and auto parts.
A girl in cut-offs sits on the hood
of a white Rambler mottled with rust.
What sent her out here into last light?
Maybe boredom or an uneasy glare.
In the moon's dim currency
the cars remember but cannot start again.

Command

The diesel engines of the big rigs
idled outside the truck stop, moths
fluttering in the parking lot lights.

I was driving across Nevada, driving east
back home to Elko County,
my first year of teaching high school.
So it was 1976 or '77,

stopped in Battle Mountain
for chicken fried steak and a beer.
It was when I went to the men's room,
the sour smell
and angry graffiti on the cinder-block wall.

I can't recall his face, he was fifty or so,
but I remember the indelible scrawl
of his voice,

My name is Cliff, and I am
The biggest asshole you've ever met.

"I wouldn't know about that," I said,
taking a step to move past him.
He leaned close and spoke,

Believe me. I'm a liar,
but I'm telling the truth now.
I'm the biggest asshole you've ever met.
Say it. I didn't want to.

Who would make such a command?
Now I know each soul
has its own underworld and particular suffering,
but I didn't want to think about the things he'd done.

He leaned into me,
Say it.

And so I said it and reached for the door,
not knowing what he would do.
He looked to the floor,
barely nodded his head, and said *Thank you.*

Breath

The resigned and restless
deep adult breaths of my parents
echoed around me,

growing up in a house of sighs
and tableaux. A silence beneath
like the underwater show
we saw when I was nine, the women

all movement and slow swirl
in their aquarium world,
all held breath and show.

Memory is green-tinged, blurred.
My father faithful
to his repeated whims —

his softened voice, his feigned
sincerity, his arm around his best friend's
wife. My mother took a breath,

held it. This was the habit
of her suffering. She kept a postcard,
a picture of those underwater swimmers,
safety-pinned to her wicker laundry basket.

Not some glimmer of Sea World
fantasy, I understand now,
not escapism but submerged anger,

practiced and slow.
A constant reminder
of rising up, a breath

held in, let go,
then sinking back down
under it.

Imperfect History

Tonight my hands trace
my body's imperfect history.
The scars, not seen but felt,
like pain remembered.
I grew up in a house of shadows:
I knew ghosts.
If this life is quick light
between two long darknesses,

then I am lonely and feel
the huge shadow of a cloud
crossing the moon, the shadow
so cold, so complete.
And then there is no moon,
no light to fall through.

Sway

A noose of moonlight—

I think I see what my father saw
that night when he went out
to the leaning barn—

he followed the light,

scared up some rope in the tack room
to toss over the beam.

The wind rending itself
through barbed fences.

I found him
the next morning,

kneeling on a hay bale, his head
in his hands,
under the dangling rope
he'd left unknotted.

Asterisks of ice on the glass.
Frozen stars to look past.

He was chilled and wretched.
The night had made a penitent of him.
Under the thrum of winter wind, his sobs.

The bay mare was unimpressed.
The rafters creaked like a boat.
Steam rising
from the yellow palace of hay bales.

The wind blows and turns
another page.

Oddly elating
to see him that way.
For the first time in years

it was easy to reach for him.
I led him back to the house,

the rope left there
swaying.

I Kneel to See the Dead Great Horned Owl

found on the shoulder of the road.
This morning its night eyes are still
open and oval as a citron moon animated
like the glass eye of a Buddha.
The owl's on its back

on a bed of red dirt—Manet's
dead matador, one wing a gray cape
thrown nakedly open
to an absence in the sky. I think of
the luff of owl wings,
the last swoop and glide
before it was struck by a truck
and slammed into its own shadow
with a plush thud in the roadside dust.

Now I regard the owl, and it
seems to regard me. The longer I look
the more I'm reminded
of Severn's pencil drawing
of the vulnerable Keats,
very peaceably asleep, forever.

Aren't the dead always waiting
to be lifted? With both hands
I take the soft bird body,
heavier, more dense
than I might have guessed,
and carry it to the car, placing the owl
next to me in the seat of the passenger.

* * *

My friend Diane makes three paintings
and one drawing of the owl in two days.
But now the yellow moons of the eyes

are eclipsed and she asks me
to take the owl, which she has kept
in the refrigerator with a head of lettuce
and rolls of film. Since I've found him
there have been odd juxtapositions,
the owl where it should not be:
on the ground, on the car seat next to me,
and now again in Diane's refrigerator.
Lettuce is to film as owl is to wind.

And so I want to put the owl where it belongs.

In a tree, I'm thinking, shouldn't an owl be
in a tree? It is an old oak—gray, weathered,
bare. But still there
on the edge of my neighbor's ranch, still the tallest thing
for miles among the sage, stunted pine and juniper.

The skewed and relic oak to which all owls in the valley
will come in their time.

Where I live, I've heard the great-horned owls
and their call that is a question.
Like the coyotes they are often heard but seldom seen.
On a windy September day I hike for an hour,
cradling the owl until I reach the bleached-gray tree.
The oak has been dead for years.
The limbs brittle
like bleached coral. Where two limbs cross
I take baling wire and twine to secure the owl,
with difficulty, upright in the tree.
The wind swaying through the grasses
sounding like the river that isn't here.

* * *

Absence has its own sound.
One day at dusk I heard it
and began to walk toward the relic oak.
Three weeks since I left the owl in the tree.

The sun was setting along the ragged ridgeline,
a bright glow like burning
paper. The low clouds were red with flame.
I skirted the old mine, its beat-up, second-hand land
where the earth is torn
inside out, a shamble of gray tailings. Then
followed the trail that zigzags
along the wash and jags across the gully
traced by summer rains. A bright
and swollen moon,
nearly full but a bit wobbly, was on the rise.

A few white asterisks began to show in the sky.
I climbed out of the ravine
and approached the tree, but was stopped
by confusions of light that puzzled
for some moments
before I realized what I was seeing.
A thousand and another thousand
feathers blown loose from the owl,

caught and leafed out
from each taloned twig and limb.
The tree was filled with feathers of silver
that pulsed and thrilled. The mind of the owl tree
was plural, every feather
a separate flight, shining to live.

2

Herida de Amor

Ah, it's been a long time, no? the waiter says.
Yes, I say, unsure. I am the only customer.
I ask for a Budweiser. You are always doing that,
he says, Here you should drink Mexican beer.

He gestures to a poster on the wall.
A woman in a dress patterned with small bright birds,
dances and holds a bottle of *Pacifico,*
the birds swirling around her.

OK, I nod. I have never been in this restaurant.
I've never seen this man who greets me.
There's the last squint of daylight
through the window. A blurred sun
burns down behind the hills.

He brings the Mexican beer, takes my order,
and sits at the table.
Do you remember the watch I used to wear? he says.
No, I say. He rolls up his sleeve,
revealing the pale outline on his brown skin
where the watch used to be.
I gave it to a woman, he says,
and now I am sad
because the watch is gone and so is she.

With his fingertips he flicks
some specks of salt from the checkered cloth.
He lowers his head, speaking softly,
Now I have all this time to think of her
and no watch.

He gets up and puts a quarter in the jukebox.
The song sung in Spanish
is a song of pain.
I hear him in the kitchen singing,
Herida de amor.

I listen and remember.
Although the woman I'm thinking of
never wore a design of birds,
I see her coming to me
in just such a dress.

I hear the sigh,
the sound the dress makes
when it slips off her body
and she steps out of it

and all those bright birds flutter down,
huddle together on the floor.
The waiter brings my order.
He looks out the window,
the feminine outline of the silhouetted hills.
It is always darkest at night, he says
without irony. And I know
what he means, know he is right.

He's not talking about the night,
but the second night, the dark
within the dark when I wake and wonder,
Where did she go?

And I am left to imagine a migration
of beautiful birds and women.
The women dancing, the birds flying around them
down in Mexico.

Then I Close My Eyes

between Morelia and Guadalajara.
The bus passes in the fallen
dark—graveyards and silent bells
in the still church towers of the towns
where women and men
and children sleep,
and where a mean and angry man
sleeps, because there is always
an angry man, and where
someone not sleeping weeps,
because there is always
someone weeping.
The bus swerves through the Sierra Madre,
the driver dodging potholes
and occasional cattle, their eyes
a red glow in the swaying headlights
as my flickering dream
bumps against the cold window glass.
In sleep I touch the ticket in my shirt pocket
to make sure it is still there.
Somewhere a long braid, a cut cord of black hair,
keepsake in a drawer. Somewhere
a scorpion waits inside the warm dark of a shoe.
Somewhere under a lean moon a lean dog shivers.
A net of stars and the vague sense
of inner weather. All the passengers on this bus,
their breath a steady sea—in motion
all of us, some are leaving
someone, and there are others,
blessed me, I am among them,
making a way, slowly making a way
through the night
toward the beloved.

Release

With their hands the boys
had caught a trout
in the shallow creek
and brought it to the water trough

where it hides in the shadow
of the curved neck of their father's roan,
as the horse bends to drink
from its own reflection. The day

is tired with troubled breathing.
The woman dreams
this not so long ago
noise of her two boys
grown, gone now to other states.

Her husband enters the room, sets his hat
on her dressing table—upside down on its crown,
to preserve the rim, to hold the luck in.

There are perfume bottles on the table,
verbena and white lilac.
Thin vials of pills from the hospital.

The woman wakes. Outside the wind
shakes leaves from the cottonwood.
The limbs creak like saddle leather.

A string of starlings
whirls then breaks apart, a snapped
strand of black beads
scattering. Another nail
torn loose from the barn. It's time

to turn to what is broken.
Things fall, the man says,
faster than he can fix them.

She coughs a mouthful of blood
in the white handkerchief
he holds to her lips.

A lifetime of hunting
and home butchering, but *this* red,
this blood weakens him.

The day and a day thirty years ago
swirl in slow current
through her room and out
the open window.

Around the worn house,
the wind trills
like boys learning to whistle.

She closes her eyes to hold
the vision in; this is a moment
of having, not loss.

The trout, a cloud in the water trough,
brushes against four walls, sways
into shadow, hovering there.

She shuts her eyes tighter,
until she grabs the cornered fish
and lifts it shining from water.

A slippery and translucent light,
twitching and flipping against air.
She cradles it,

takes a long breath and divines the way,
traces the green scent of wild mint
to the living river that shivers
like muscle beneath the skin.

Kneeling, she lets go,
releases it—a life, all that leap and fight—
following what follows
back into the scrolled stream.

What I Believed

Today I brought home a rock
found on the Lake Tahoe shore.
The water has worn
into the rock a face.

I hold it in my hand and think back
to what I believed in my youth:
if I skipped a flat stone
across the skin of the lake
the stone would sing the shape of wind
and water.

And if late at night
I stood under the wandering light of stars
beneath a certain second-story window
near Dayton, Nevada, and took a pebble
and tossed it up and let it click
against the dark glass, the face of a girl
would appear in the black square above.

She'd come out to me and we'd cross the field
through the sweet reek of wet hay
to the neighbor's barn where the horses
were restless with our presence.
It was there that I came to regard
sex as a large, nervous animal.

The girl's father didn't understand
how the flowers were wrecked
beneath his daughter's window,
the broken tiger lilies I'd stepped on.
Afterwards, we laughed that he was so upset,
but maybe those bright lilies
stood for something he believed in.

In the barn, when I lit the votive candle
I'd brought to light the musky dark,
we saw the powder on my jeans,
vivid-orange where my thighs had brushed
the pollen-laden stems of the taller flowers.
Later, I thought the shape of shadows
trembled with the pitch of our excitement.

In the twisting light of candle flame,
she read the smooth skin
of my face with her fingers.
I wouldn't guess
what time could do.
I think I thought I was already
who I was going to be.
Not knowing yet
that the years would shape, change,
and reveal me.

American Flat

Under the high hunger of hawks,
I've been walking in Nevada.
In the republic of sage where
shoe leather and femurs of cows
    endure.

Before the sun lifts to its full height,
before the cattle, mapped with white,
    follow their plodding thirst
to drink from the quiet water,
I hike to my platonic pond.

Each morning I stand in the same place
and find in reflection a different sky:
another flock of clouds go by, different
light in the tree, different scatter of leaves
    on the water, another me.

A twig floating on the minnow waves,
my secret boat. Tomorrow
    this day will be
a blue lupine I've picked and pressed
between pages of a wildflower guide.

I'll walk the path again. Trace
    and retrace. Let the dust
rise up and fall among my footsteps.
Let the calm coil inside itself like a rope.
Let the days heal more than they erode.

Nesting

I haven't yet removed the tangle
of red hair from the brush she used,
but I pulled and dragged our old bed
down the stairs and out the door.

Thought I'd borrow a truck
and haul the mattress away—stains,
memories, all of it.

What's that song?
Early morning, the birds talking up the light,
bright house finch tune,
a loose disjointed warble.

On long walks
on the dust path through chaparral,
she'd point to the compact nests,
little cups in a juniper bush.

The materials of nest building
are usually the remains of something else.

Now the ruckus of finches.
How they shrill and bicker,
male and female tearing apart
the mattress batting with their blunt bills.

Small birds winging by with white wadding
like ragged snowflakes in their beaks.
They'll build nests throughout the valley.

"Where are you going?" I'd call
when she'd get up from our bed,
even when it was just down the hall and back.

Once she had me see out the window
to the night. The shadow shapes
of two wild horses, the blue blur
of their silhouettes, drifting through
two moons of breath on the cold, glazed glass.

They looked like boats floating past,
the bulky prow of their heads.
We named them —

Wander On and *Big Blue Lonesome.*
At night there is such huge movement
in the dark—horses, ships,
memory. Back in bed,

I traced the scar above her right eyebrow, the pink
crescent moon she said she'd tell me about
someday and never did.

Perseid Shower

Meteors break
through the late-summer night,

white blossoms scattering, furiously.
They don't make a noise,

at least none
that we can hear.

They disappear in all directions—
signifying desire

and its difficulty.
There. The half-moon floats

thin and translucent
as an insect's wing. We say the moon is

half-full,
even as it wanes.

So much longing . . .
to witness the unfolding

across distance. How we must look
to anyone watching.

Here is the star cage.
Here the still life with black clock.

Magpies in the Graveyard

They are not beautiful,
although their blacker feathers glimmer
like rainbow oil in the sun.
Yin-yang birds, black/white
with a long tail. Flash
of white patch with each wing-beat.
We say a murder of crows. A covey of quail.
But I can't recall
the term for many magpies.
A cemetery of magpies. A sunrise of them.
I'm here this morning
because I want to be lonely
among the tombstones—the dates and names.
It takes one beating heart
to make a magpie, two wings,
four thousand feathers, a handful
of fluted and hollow bones.
One flies and the others follow.
Listen. The surprising flutter.
They rise like an undulating road
of magpies, black with white dashes, they lift
like prayer into the blank graveyard air.
Something into nothing.

Teaching Poetry to 3rd Graders

At recess a boy ran to me
with a pink rubber ball and asked
if I would kick it to him. He handed me the ball,
then turned and ran
and ran and ran, not turning back
until he was far out in the field.
I wasn't sure I could kick the ball
that far. But I tried,
launching a perfect and lucky kick.
The ball sailed in a beautiful arc
about eight stories high,
landed within a few feet of the 3rd grader
and took a big bounce off the hard playground dirt.
Pleased, I turned to enter the school building.
And then (I don't know where they came from
so quickly) I heard a rumbling behind me
full tilt. They were carrying pink balls and yellow balls
of different sizes, black and white checkered
soccer balls. They wanted me to kick for them.
And now this is a ritual—this is how we spend recess.
They stand in line, hand me the ball and run.
The balls rise like planets
and the 3rd graders
circle dizzily beneath the falling sky,
their arms outstretched.

* * *

In class the kids are making similes and I write them
on the board as they call out—
A river swishing like a horse's tail.
Smooth as a window, quiet as pain.
The rain clattering like a spilled jar of marbles.
Then a wave of laughter sweeps the room.
In my new shoes I must have shuffled
across the school carpet rife with static.
My hair is standing straight up
as if I'm a shocked cartoon character
or a scared and cornered cat.
When I write on the chalkboard,
blue sparks fly from my hand
to the metal strip that frames the green.
Everything I touch crackles.
When I help a student at her desk,
a yellow four-inch arc of lightning streaks
from my hand to hers, shocking the pencil from her grip.
The students watch amazed. "Pick up the pencil!" I say,
"Don't be afraid."

* * *

(A note found on the playground
pinned by wind against the chain-link fence)

From: Daniel A.
To: Missy

In case you guest
  I love you   it is a presant
    to see you.
        When I dreem.
    I dreem you   Not gold
  not a cristal pond   not a bird
    singing evry song
      you ever herd   jus you
          Only.   None else

Because I love you
      and love to say your name
    I saw you
      and remem ber this
    Thanks you for a dreem

      Who?   can take
        Your plase

3

Sheep and Stars

The sheep see the world as meadow,
some chaparral to cross, the clattering
over rimrock, loose shale and scree
to reach the grass and the creek,
snowmelt to drink.
              I'd see
the sheep trail, thousands of pellet droppings,
the shepherd's footprints in the dirt.
Then at the watering holes—
statuettes of sheep
                      sculpted from mud,
a blurred thumbprint
in the neck or shank of the figurines.
I walked at dusk.
You wouldn't think
a thousand lamb-ewe pairs, a shepherd and his dogs
would be hard to find. But in two weeks
of hiking through the valley and mountain draws,
just droppings, tracks,
and small flocks of mud sheep.

   * * *

When I finally meet Elvis Montes
we walk back to his travel trailer:
a *ristra* of hanging sheep hooves,
threaded with leather,
                    a clicking wind-chime.
Three walking sticks
                carved from cottonwood limbs
near the door—sheep, stars, moons
and mountains inscribed in the wood,
a rattlesnake skin nailed to a board,
two candles and several mud sheep on the windowsill.
Inside the trailer photographs
of his wife and daughters in Peru—

his three-year contract in Nevada about to end,
he will finally go back
and for the first time see his youngest child.
                                        He shows me
his pencil drawings: rocks, a porcupine quill
removed from the nose of his dog,
a red-tail-hawk feather finely depicted,
the weathered leg-bone of a cow.
I tell him the drawings seem felt, not seen.
He doesn't look at the objects
                        when he sketches. He says,
I hold them with my eyes closed
and then I draw from . . .
                        He pauses.
I try to fill in the word. "Touch," I say,
trying to help. "Memory?"
Faith, he says.

* * *

Sheep in a meadow.
From here the sheep look cottony.
                        Elvis walks my way,
a strange corsage of pink flesh
wrapped around his wrist and secured with leather strips.
It smells of camphor. I consider
                        how he tied it
with one hand.
The underside of his wrist
was torn by thorns
as he worked a tangled lamb free
from the bramble of wild roses
along the cutbank of the creek.
                        "What do you have on it?" I ask.
He pulls a jar from his front jeans pocket,
a skinned rattlesnake in liniment.

"Snake oil," I say,
but Elvis doesn't get my joke. *Yes,* he says seriously.
Who is closer to the land than a snake?
It is come from the earth and it will quiet the wound.

His clothes
have the scent of wild mint
he must have waded through
to reach the caught lamb.

* * *

Through the long draw of the canyon,
following the sheep and watching the old dog.
A blue heeler eager to please, who limps

when she walks
with blood-caked paws and a ruined hip,
and who now runs and darts expertly
herding some woolly strays back to the flock.
Above us clouds roll by like blue smoke.
"Hey Elvis," I say, because I get a kick
out of saying "Hey Elvis."
"Look at that sky. Are you ever afraid
it will rain and your sheep will shrink?"
He just shakes his head.

We walk on
talking about his return to Peru,
the mother and brother
we each have lost.
I recite Sylvia Plath's poem for him,

"Sheep in Fog,"
"People or stars
regard me sadly, I disappoint them."
And Elvis mishears the lines as

Sheep or stars . . .
I disappoint them. He is tremendously moved.

* * *

The sheep settled in the afternoon heat,
we hike to the creek beneath the willow, strip down
to wade in and I think of when
I cast the fine dust
              that was my mother
upon this water. Her ashes in sunlight,
                    silvering
and swirling, a picture-book galaxy.
Some of the ashes seemed not to fall at all,
                    but sparked
and blinked out in air like blown stars.
"Hey Elvis, this is where
my mother's ashes are scattered," I say,
not sure how he will react.
               Here? he says,
pointing to the water. "Yes, here."
Then he dips his entire body into the deepest part of the creek,
and when he emerges diamonds drip
from his face and hair.
He gives me a shove
and I'm underwater. Looking down
the length of my body and watching
the faint glow of Elvis floating away,
I see that we are made of light. I rise up
              and break
the surface, glittering.

* * *

Tonight there's a quiet that listens.
The creek calm, glassed over with moonlight,
                glistening
still. I think of Elvis out there
with his two thousand sheep and his four thousand stars.

The whorl of the Milky Way a blurred thumbprint.

At our last meal
we ate lamb and tasted it —
sun and wind, sage
and juniper, the spring green
meadow, the smell of mountains after rain.
We tasted memory.
There's an effacement
of what was,
what the wind dries up and blows away.
Here in Nevada we say,
"Dust
isn't what it used to be."
Sometimes
when walking a windblown slope,
I find a cairn of hand-stacked stones.
Elvis signaling the way
to stands of aspen, spring-fed creeks,
bright grass and watering holes
where I'll find
a small flock of mud sheep
shaped from faith.

4

Frame Blue

I watch him, knee-deep in the evening lyric
  of the Truckee River, a fly-fisherman
    imagining trout,

the light bending
  into the river. The trout sees
    through its window of water,

the fraudulent mayfly—wings
  tricked from plastic,
    red teardrops on the tip

of a cedar waxwing's feather
  made into eyes.
    An intricate and pretty lie.

"Beyond the shadow
  of a trout," my father used to say.
    He also said,

"Trout live in the nicest places."
  When he broke his silence to charm
    or seduce, my father said a lot of things.

* * *

Our neighbor Roy Hawks rode up on horseback
and said a mountain lion had killed a calf. I was too young
to do anything except watch my dad and several men

gallop off in a posse that tracked the cat into the next valley.
I imagined it—a tawny light, color of late-summer hills,
moving through the low brush

and over slickrock. The dogs treed the animal
in a ponderosa pine, the mountain lion hunched on a limb.
When my father on horseback, tried to take a photograph,

the first shot clicked by mistake,
and caught only blue Nevada sky. I remember
photographs of the lion,

but it was the sky
that my dad had enlarged—9 x 12, nothing but pure blue
hanging on the wall in his study.

The blue within the frame
changing tone and hue, the shifting
light and dark of my father's moods.

* * *

I had my own blue object of affection.

A globe
that glowed with the flick of a light switch.
At night I gazed
across the black space of my room.
Earth—my favorite planet.
I fell asleep in the light of the bright world.

* * *

One night there was a fight
that woke me, my mother's voice
different, more shrill than I'd ever heard it—
something about a fishing trip that was not
a fishing trip. Something about motel bills
and *that* woman.

The world unraveled like a peel
in one long blue spiral.
And though my mother didn't go outside for a week,
she couldn't hide

from me, the cut lip, the blue bruise
going to yellow on her cheek.
It changed the way I looked at his hands.

* * *

My mother's hands.
We visited her childhood friend. They hadn't seen each other
    for a long time.
Ella asked her to play the piano.

I didn't know my mother played,
and so I sat next to her
on the piano bench. Watched her transform

all those busy busy black notes on the sheet music
into beauty. Ella said,
"Oh, Aldora, I always loved the way you played."

My mom pulled the wooden cover down like a coffin lid
    over the keys.
She put her hands on the casement, spread them out to make
    a silent chord.
"That was a long time ago," she said.

* * *

The trapped coyote.

He told the story so often
that my mother and I could see it—a paw,
the flesh, ragged and raw, caught.
And the three-legged track limping away.

* * *

The boy is eight or nine.
His father has him hold the phone.
"If a man answers," the father instructs his son,
"ask for your friend Clayton.
If a woman answers, don't say anything.
Just give it to me."
A woman answers and the boy surrenders the phone.
The father grabs it and shoos the boy from the room.
But not before the boy hears
the father's voice, soft and velvet,
and knows that this would hurt his mother.

* * *

A plain blue square of silence.
How the blue was framed and interior.
How the man would sit for an hour
quiet as the wreath of cigarette smoke
that swirled around his head.
The flat square of only blue—

no mountain lion in a tree,
no wife, no gliding
red-tailed hawk. No me.

* * *

There was a time when I adored him.
He tried to tease me out of my quiet.
"Little boy with a cloud inside him," he said.

And he told the story of Jackie Robinson
breaking the color line,
so movingly that I became a Dodger fan.

He quit the Elks Club when Ernie Wong was denied membership.
He looked out for and gave food, clothes, and money
to the family of a Mexican ranch worker.

* * *

My sweet brother, Luke, left me twice—
when he went away to college
and when he died.

He was never mean to me, not once,
and though he was twelve years older, when we played
he played my equal.

In a game of tag on the park grass I fell
exhausted and for the first time felt my own racing
heart in the middle of me. I didn't even know

I had a heart, this pounding, and was frightened.
But my brother calmed me. "Don't worry," he said,
"It's just your heart. It's what you think with."

* * *

In autumn my father would curse the cottonwood.
The oldest and tallest thing around, it grew beside the cutbank,
its roots and leaves clogging the shallow watercourse

between the two biggest ponds where the cattle drank.
Luke loved the tree and it was his protest that kept it
from being cut down, even after he'd left the ranch.

* * *

Disguised as himself my father hid
in silence, sitting in the study

with the framed blue on the wall,
the mantel clock banging every 15 minutes.
Sometimes he would stand on the porch
looking out on the actual blue.
Once I stepped out before I knew he was there
and found myself next to him.
I was a teenager.
We were already settled
into a dialogue of silence.
I could hear the crinkle of his cigarette,
then his exhale, a sigh like a fugue.
Our dual shadows were two mute spires.

The land ran out into the space of things unsaid.
I sensed a difference
between distance and solitude,
but I didn't know what it was.

* * *

Not long after my brother's funeral,
my father took a chainsaw to the tree.
My mom had asked him not to cut it down. She said

she liked to look out the window and see it and think of Luke.
For weeks my father bucked and split the wood, the heavy maul
    ringing off the steel wedge.
He stacked the wood four feet high and made a wall.

* * *

My mother knew the worst things about my father—
in that way, they had an intimacy.
When my mom revealed her cancer to me,

actually showed me her ravaged breast, I realized
how alone my mother had been with her body.
She let herself die,

telling no one until she was beyond help.
When I asked her why, she said,
"It's my life and I didn't want this to be his."

Shortly after she died, my father said to me,
"Why did she do that?
I could have had her another ten years."

* * *

Something lost
to the trap, but something
gained, the moment of separation.
The heart leaping with animal pain and then

the broken run into the open.

* * *

My father sold the house and land.
Seventy-two years old he bought
a condo in California
and a big purple truck.

He dyed his hair metallic gold.
So many things got lost—
the dog, bank accounts,
family albums, the blue sky photograph,

my mother's occasional journals. I pressed him about
    the journals.

"I got rid of all that crap," he said,
"Do you want that?" He pointed to a tin

on the lowest shelf
of the new
home-entertainment center.
My mother's ashes.

* * *

I knew then that in death I would finally separate them.
I would give my mother to the water,
and when it was time, my father to the dirt.

* * *

He phoned me to say he'd be gone two weeks
to play in a tennis tournament in Mexico.
"A tennis tournament?" I said.

I had never known him to play tennis.
The next time I visited there was a tall tennis trophy
with my father's name on it.

I poked around and looked for a racquet or balls. Nothing.
I asked my dad if he would like to play some tennis.
"No, I don't think so," he replied.

Not a fortune,
but a considerable amount of money
was going fast. I asked him about this.

He said he had read an article
in the local paper. A little girl with leukemia.
He'd gone to the hospital to visit her and met her family.

He was helping to pay for her treatment.
"Well, this is remarkable generosity," I said,
"I'd like to meet the girl and her family."
"I don't think that will be possible," he said.

I told my girlfriend that it might be a difficult day,
but I wanted her to meet my father.
We drove over the Sierra for a visit.

When we arrived my father came out to the car.
I was struggling to get a plant from the backseat
that we had brought as a gift.

When I stood to make introductions, the Boston fern
    in my hands,
my father said, "I've been thinking
I should disinherit you."

He phoned when I was at an arts colony in New Hampshire.
"Oh, this is terrible," my father said.
"What happened now?"

"There was an earthquake yesterday
and I was downtown and a brick wall collapsed on the truck.
Insurance won't cover it and I'm going to have to ask you

for five thousand." When we hung up, I considered the truck
and the natural disaster and I called
the office of my father's county sheriff

and asked if there had been an earthquake there.
"No," the man said, "No earthquake.
Why are you asking?"

I explained that I had a relative who was trying to con me
for $5,000. "Who is it?" the man asked. "My father," I said.
"I'm sorry," the man said.

* * *

And finally the father granted a kindness
which was to allow the son to watch over him
when he was weak. To wash his face

and to shave him, to help him back to bed.
To rub his back and touch him
the last night his body would be a body.

I pulled the sheet and blanket
up around him.
"Gary," he said, "Can I

ask you just *one* question?"
It occurred to me that this might be
our last conversation—

some Shakespearean pronouncement
of contrition, some accounting
to be made.

"Yes," I said.
And then he spoke, "Gary,
what's a bistro?"

* * *

Some of what my father said
    were simply pretty lies. Some
        of the women he lied to

were pretty. Some of what he said
    was true. Sometimes
        I stand by the river

thinking about water, thinking about
   what there was
      to learn from my father—

how to fish, how to lie. A few
   swallows dip and glide, glide
      and dip above the Truckee. This is

one of the nicest places. Lucky
   or unlucky trout. They live
      in a stream,

they live in a fisherman's dream.
   If the trout bites,
      it will leap, hungry and with hope.

* * *

When I woke in the next morning
there was silence. Nothing
could be more quiet.
I found him in death
a figure of penitence and pity.
He had died in a posture of prayer,
falling to his knees or trying to crawl,
his clasped hands on the bed mimicking
childhood's invocation, *Now I lay me down . . .*

His face was not at peace,
but startled, the eyes
staring out of the blue into the blue.
There was a mustiness in the room,
his skin coated with a sheen of dampness
like the page of a book left outside all night;
his mouth already puckered with stiffness,
his familiar pout.

With my hand I mothered the shock of gray hair
from his forehead.
I called 911. "This is not an emergency,"
I said, "but I have found
my father dead."
I held the phone to my ear.
The voice on the line commanded that I press my finger
against his throat to find a pulse.

Tell me what you feel, the voice said.
Oh, he was dead. So dead
I didn't want to hurt him.
I reached around his neck
to the carotid artery—if you had seen us there—
the sad son of a sad father,
my hands around his throat
trying to discern
just what it was I felt.

I think he would have wanted
me to touch him tenderly,
to touch his brow once and lay a hand
upon his forehead.
He would have liked to have been loved.
The voice in my ear demanding
What do you feel? What do you feel?
My father was dead.
Forgiveness, I almost said.

* * *

But I didn't forgive him.
I buried him instead.